A Grownup's Guide to Living a Young-at-Heart Life

T0025891

A Grownup's Guide to Living a Young-at-Heart Life

From the Littlest Experts
Who Live It Everyday

DAVID HELLER AND
SALLY MELZER

To order additional copies of this book, contact:
Xlibris
1-888-795-4274
www.Xlibris.com
Orders@Xlibris.com
657847

XLIBRIS BOOKS BY DAVID HELLER

THE SOUL OF A RELATIONSHIP:
200 Practical Reflections On Finding,
Nurturing and Revitalizing Love (2014)

**PEOPLE GO CRAZY OVER LOVE LIKE
BEES GO WILD OVER HONEY:**
Children on Romance, Dating and Kissing (2014)

**THE 200 MOST IMPORTANT THINGS
KIDS NEED TO KNOW ABOUT LIFE**
(And A Parent Needs To Teach Them) - with Jared Heller (2014)

FRIENDSHIP IS LIKE LOVE WITH MORE LETTERS IN IT:
Children's Colorful Views of Friendship -
with David Johns (2014)

**IF MY MOM AND DAD HAD SAILED ON
THE MAYFLOWER, THAT 'OL
SHIP WOULD HAVE SUNK!**
Kids' Views of American History (2014)

DEDICATION

TO OUR BELOVED MOTHER AND SISTER,

BLANCHE HELLER,

WHO COLLECTED DOLLS, ENJOYED

TRIVIA CONTESTS, AND LOVED

FINDING TOYS FOR HER GRANDCHILDREN

AND NIECES - - -

SHE REMAINS

IN OUR HEARTS FOREVER YOUNG.

INTRODUCTION

If the reader is anticipating an optimistic book you would be correct. Being young-at-heart means many things to many people, but it most certainly means to everyone a wish to celebrate life. Franz Kafka once wrote: "Youth is the ability to see beauty. Anyone who maintains the ability to see beauty never grows old." Indeed, the possibility of being young-at-heart is open to everyone, regardless of age or position in life. But what is required in practical terms to achieve and sustain a youthful perspective on life and the world?

Enter the experts. Four to thirteen year-old aficionados of exuberance and vitality, children will have much to teach the rest of us about how to be light-hearted and merry. In fact, a young-at-heart demeanor comes quite naturally to most youngsters. This special quality is so often intrinsic in childhood that it makes one wonder why so many of us lose sight of it along the way. It certainly can only inspire us, instruct us and bemuse us to eavesdrop on children as they discuss what it means to be truly young-at-heart.

There are a plethora of topics related to being youthful that children will address with alacrity, all with the educational and socialization needs of grownups in mind. Initially, the children offers views on what being old-at-heart means and then move on to some precise and colorful definitions of being young-at-heart. The kids describe in animated fashion some of the behaviors and attitudes they consider young-at-heart.

Then in a more prescriptive posture, the youngsters expound on how to get more out of life -- advice for all ages. Concluding on a more philosophical note, they remind us that the world is a better place when more of its citizens try to be young-at-heart.

Fairy tales, chocolates and cotton candy, amusement parks, baseball and major league portions of love and fun -- all are in the mix in the children's responses as the young-at-heart phenomenon is captured for your edification and enjoyment. The children are really quite intuitive as they sense we are all seekers, attempting to restore and advance the lightheartedness in our everyday lives.

David Heller, Ph.D. and Sally Melzer

**LET'S START BY DEFINING A FEW THINGS:
WHAT ARE SOME EXAMPLES OF BEHAVIOR
THAT YOU CONSIDER TO BE OLD-AT-HEART?**

"Yellin' at kids because their ball went on your lawn." (Pierce, age 10)

"Chewing tobacco and spittin' it at people." (Robert, age 11)

"Saying kids are a burden and not much more." (Seily, age 9)

"Not being interested in cooking yummy food." (Lana, age 8)

"Saying that fun and games are just for kids." (Amanda, age 9)

"Believing that children can't tell the truth about people, whether they're nice or not..... We always know." (Jocelyn, age 11)

"Not learning to use chopsticks for Chinese food!" (Karl, age 10)

"Never buying M & M's." (Evan, age 7)

"Not having any dreams." (Charlotte, age 12)

"Never traveling and not being curious about the world." (Jared, age 13)

SO WHAT DOES IT MEAN TO BE "YOUNG-AT-HEART"?

"It's being a middle of the ages person and saying: 'I don't give a hoot! I'm going to play kickball today!'" (Ron, age 10)

"Never missing taking one of the free lollipops from the bank." (Cara, age 9)

"It's getting on the floor and playing Legos with kids." (Benny, age 6)

"It's when you try on a new red dress even though you are ninety-one!" (Dina, age 8)

"It's when you believe that romance is not just for teenagers." (Mae, age 11)

"When you only have one dime left in your pocket. but that doesn't stop you from putting it in the bubble gum machine...... Unless the bubble gum costs a quarter. Then you're in trouble." (Connie, age 8)

"It's when you go back for seconds and thirds on being a child again." (Lili, age 11)

"Young-at-heart means you don't have to worry about little things -- like how many stocks and bonds you have," (Gil, age 11)

"A person is a kid-at-heart when your heart says to your mind: 'Say, Mind, go get me some popcorn with lots of butter in it..... And make it the whole bucket size'." (Ethan, age 11)

"It doesn't hurt to be a little mischievous if you want to be young-at-heart." (Eleanor, age 9)

"It means you can't stand cruelty of any kind...... Even to ants, because they might have feelings too." (Dylan, age 7)

"It's when you are seventy-five and you still want to play touch football and call out the plays..... Of course you might have trouble hearing what you call out." (Jerrold, age 11)

"Young-at-heart means living life good while you can, it's having a good time while you are alive...... I've heard it's a lot harder later on." (Martin, age 9)

"Young-at-heart means you are full of laughter and full of something special called love." (Gregory, age 9)

LET'S ESTABLISH CREDENTIALS
ON WHY CHILDREN ARE THE ULTIMATE EXPERTS
ON HOW TO BE YOUNG-AT-HEART

"Because we're geniuses like Einstein when
it comes to fun!" (Brett, age 10)

"We are born having fun and it's our job to act young and
show everybody else how to laugh." (Cameron, age 9)

"Joy is our middle name." (Peter, age 10)

"Eating sugar cereals keeps us young-at-heart." (Bob, age 7)

"We're smaller and we see the small things in life
that other people miss." (Delia, age 9)

"Kids are kids every day of the week. Grown-ups aren't.
They need to go back in time." (Carey, age 8)

"We've seen a lot of young-at-heart movies, so we know what it takes....... To be young- at-heart, it takes liking to feel real happy at a funny movie or real scared at a scary movie." (Erin, age 12)

"We learn about it at camp every single summer...... Grown-ups should go to camp." (Ron, age 10)

"Personally, I think it's because kids are basically brilliant about everything and adults are too thick-headed!" (Eleanor, age 9)

"Playgrounds keep us young and also they are good for exercise and playing with new friends." (Mitchell, age 7)

"To be an expert at young-at-heart stuff, all you really need is a room full of toys..... Most of us have that by the time we're four." (Holly, age 6)

WHAT IS THE BIGGEST DIFFERENCE
BETWEEN A PERSON WHO IS
YOUNG-AT-HEART AND
A PERSON WHO IS NOT?

"The size of their heart." (Richard, age 10)

"The young-at-heart person plays with toy cars and
the other ones don't do that." (Benny, age 6)

"The person who isn't cares a ton about money and the person
who is young-at-heart cares more about love." (Cheryl, age 9)

"Guess which one would rather play tag?" (Dina, age 8)

"The ones who aren't have no time for children." (Joe, age 8)

"Young-at-heart people love babies more than anything else...... even
a little more than chocolate, but that's good too." (Alana, age 8)

"Young-at-heart people can enjoy a baseball game even
if their team is in last place." (Tom, age 11)

"Scrious brussel sprout eaters are not young-at-heart." (Bruce, age 10)

"If one of the people is bald, he might be too
depressed to be young-at-heart." (Josh, age 8)

"The young-at-heart person will treasure their memories as
much as the things they own now." (Samantha, age 10)

"Us young-at-heart people like old-fashioned root beer..... We
don't get all excited over Coke ads." (Sara Leigh, age 10)

"The young-at-heart person will do good for people of all ages; the
other type just lays around and thinks of themselves." (Gil, age 11)

"If you are young-at-heart, you don't even care
if your sox match!" (Bonita, age 9)

"The person who isn't young acting will have a grouchy
personality and say 'darn' a whole lot." (Patrick, age 10)

"The person who is not young in spirit will have bad eyesight
from staring at a computer all day." (David, age 11)

"A young-at-heart person doesn't complain about life....
The other kind just acts like a hundred people owe them
something and nobody is paying up." (Randy, age 10)

"When you're young-at-heart, the smiles just
give it away." (Bogdan, age 11)

**WHAT IS THE BIGGEST OBSTACLE IN
THE WORLD TO POSSESSING
A YOUTHFUL ATTITUDE TOWARD
LIFE?**

"Having a pebble in your shoe." (Josh, age 6)

"Being too cautious and never jumping across rocks in a stream." (Kyle, age 10)

"Medical problems like having headaches from worrying about doing your income tax." (Miles, age 12)

"Always being worried about the future...... You shouldn't hurry up the future." (Jenn, age 12)

"Being an engineer..... All that planning makes you tired, my dad says." (Evan, age 9)

"Having a flaky head...... Too much white stuff makes you itch and you can't have fun." (Jason, age 10)

"Younger snotnoses who call you 'old'..... Don't let those troublemakers get you down." (Landon, age 11)

"Backaches and no one to rub you." (Samantha, age 10)

"Pouting so much it leaves you with a permanent face condition." (Emma, age 9)

"Believing that you are over the hill..... Once you believe you're old, you'll act that way for sure!" (Jonathan, age 10)

"Being too dignified is the biggest obstacle to being young-at-heart....... It's too boring." (Maureen, age 9)

"Feeling like you are too old to chew bubblegum...... If you have no teeth like my grandfather, that's different." (Harry, age 7)

"Suits and uncomfortable clothes like ties..... The best kind of clothes are boat clothes because they are comfortable and they let you pretend you are captain of your own ship." (Brendan, age 9)

"Being afraid to spend too much time in nature....... Mountain climbing and hang gliding and looking for bears can make you feel young again.... Plus, if you do see a bear, it will make you run faster than you ever did when you were young!" (Peter, age 10)

"The biggest obstacle is being interested in too much success instead of just having a good time." (Jacques, age 11)

"Your brain can get in the way...... It can tell you are too old to do fun things, and that keeps you from doing them." (Jared, age 13)

**CAN ANYONE BE YOUNG-AT-HEART,
NO MATTER WHAT AGE YOU ARE?**

"Yes, as long as you can tell knock-knock jokes." (Benny, age 6)

"Babies have to train for it first. At the beginning, they cry and complain too much to be young-at-heart." (Ryan, age 7)

"It's harder for middle-aged people......... They get frustrated and get all caught up with how their kids don't listen to them and are going to turn into monsters or street cleaners or gym teachers." (Jalen, age 10)

"About twenty-five year old is when it stops....... Then the people get more serious, which if you want my opinion is a huge waste of time!" (Mark, age 8)

"You shouldn't be too embarrassed if you are thirty-nine and still playing with soldiers and tanks...... The guys on the Joint Army Chiefs that give advice to the President do that too." (Scott R., age 11)

"It's a free country so there's no law that says you can't act like a kid any old time you want." (Janet, age 11)

"Anyone can be that way, as long as you can enjoy seeing a full moon and the stars at night." (Julian, age 9)

"Since I act like a grown-up when I watch my baby sister, I don't see why a grown-up can't act like a kid!" (Rosalind, age 8)

"It's never too late...... People should remember you can always go back to a playground like you're a child, and swing until the sun goes down." (Maureen, age 8)

"Well, it's easier if you're a kid because you have all the right stuff, but I could teach you if you want to pay for lessons." (Frankie, age 10)

"You will be young-at-heart as long as you keep a piece of your childhood with you when you start your first day of work." (Peyton, age 9)

"If you go bowling every Wednesday with the Gutter Girls Bowling Team, you'll stay young-at-heart at any age..... They always have a great time." (Kara, age 8)

"Just remember this: you are never too old to imagine things and you are never too old to dream about the future." (Claudia, age 11)

"Anyone can be that if they really want to...... Anyone with a good heart can be young-at- heart." (Jared, age 13)

THE CHILDREN'S TOP TEN LIST OF YOUNG-AT-HEART THINGS TO SAY

1.   "I feel like sleeping in a treehouse." (Larry, age 7)

2.   "Let's roll in the leaves and feel like it's really October." (Chanelle, age 10)

3.   "Don't work so hard. Play a lot more." (Ron, age 8)

4.   "A milkshake a day is good for you." (Mark, age 8)

5.   "I'm going to dress up for Halloween as a zebra even though I am thirty-six years old!" (Quinn, age 11)

6. "I'm not getting old, I am just sliding down the fun hill of life!" (Elizabeth, age 11)

7. "Age isn't everything; good jokes should count for something." (Trevor, age 12)

8. "Don't eat spinach or you'll turn green." (Seth, age 9)

9. "I don't care if I'm not perfect..... Scooby-Doo's neck is too big for him and look at what a big star he is." (Michael, age 9)

10. "Yolo, yolo........ Do you know what that stands for? You Only Live Once." (Jared, age 13)

**AND A FEW OTHER NOTEWORTHY
YOUNG-AT-HEART THINGS
TO SAY:**

11.   "Boy, it sure is a beautiful morning out. Today is the first day of the rest of my childhood, and I'm going to make the most out of it." (Samantha, age 10)

12.   "Thank God for another beautiful day and this life of mine." (Rebecca, age 12)

13.   "The world is one big many-colored ball and we all make up the colors on it." (Toby, (age 10)

14.   "I am going to spread a little love today." (Deidre, age 9)

THE BOTTOM TEN:
THINGS THAT PEOPLE SAY THAT ARE
DEFINITELY NOT YOUNG-AT-HEART

1. "I'm so old I could make Santa Claus look like a kid." (Tim, age 9)

2. "I'm proud of being a couch potato..... Where's my beer?" (Bruce, age 10)

3. "My best years are behind me..... and so are my best days." (Evie, age 11)

4. "Let me take a few minutes to tell you about my aches and pains." (Cheryl, age (age 10)

5. "Cleaning the dishes is a big responsibility........ and yes, it's a kid's responsibility." (Bonnie, age 8)

6.   "Hurry, hurry, hurry........ Hurry up!" (Carey, age 8)

7.   "Young people are silly and foolish." (Jasmine, age 8)

8.   "Youth is wasted on the young....... Everybody who says that is afraid to act young." (Elizabeth, age 11)

9.   "Sometimes you feel like a pigeon, sometimes you feel like a statue...... I feel like a statue." (Gil, age 11)

10.   "Life is just one very big grind." (Evan, age 9)

**AND SOME HONORABLE MENTION OFFERINGS THAT
DIDN'T QUITE MAKE
THE BOTTOM TEN LIST**

11.   "Pizza is no good for you." (Mark, age 8)

12.   "There is no way I can do that. No sir, I can't!" (Brendan, age 9)

13.   "Vacations are for the young. I am going to stay here and play a video game." (Alexis, age 12)

14.   "I can't do this. I am too old to go on a hike. I'll watch television instead." (Jared, age 13)

NOW IF YOU ARE TRULY AMONG
THE YOUNG-AT-HEART,|
THESE ARE A FEW OF THE THINGS
THAT SHOULD SEEM EMINENTLY
TRIVIAL TO YOU

"Taxes." (Mitchell, age 11)

"Having to wait at a red light." (Janna, age 11)

"Time and age." (Jared, age 13)

"Mirrors..... You shouldn't need to look at
them all the time." (Naomi, age 11)

"If your cell phone can't get reception." (Jimmy, age 9)

"If your brother gets more of something than you do.....
You shouldn't have to complain." (Aliya, age 4)

"Losing your umbrella." (Christine, age 8)

"A dull husband...... You can't let that get you down." (Eleanor, age 9)

"A few itsy bitsy measly gray hairs shouldn't
make you scream!" (Anna, age 8)

"How late the mail always comes." (Randy, age 10)

"You shouldn't get upset if you can't find a babysitter and you have a
whole family outing with the five kids instead!" (Samantha, age 10)

"Whether it's Saturday or Wednesday or any ol' day...... When you're
young-at-heart, even Mondays are good days." (Barbara, age 10)

"Money just won't seem that important to you........ I have
to admit, it hurt to say that!" (Alejandro, age 10)

**REST ASSURED, A YOUNG-AT-HEART
VIEW OF LIFE WILL RENDER THESE THINGS
VITALLY IMPORTANT**

"Seashells and sandcastles." (Eleanor, age 9)

"Having Tom Brady's rookie card." (Emmanuel, age 10)

"Sushi." (Jared, age 13)

"Chocolate, chocolate and more chocolate." (Debra, age 8)

"Sunny days...... But not too much humidity please...... Even young-at-heart people don't like to sweat if they don't have to." (Clayton, age 9)

"A jar full of pennies...... Pennies add up and you can buy jawbreakers with them." (Michael, age 5)

"People who dress up like giant peanuts and give you free samples." (Steven, age 7)

"Museums where they let you touch stuff and they don't yell at you for doing it." (Evan, age 9)

"People who are friendly because they want to be, not just 'cuz they have to be!" (Elizabeth, age 11)

"Being close to water and nature." (Leigh, age 10)

"Being grateful for what you have." (Constance, age 8)

"Treating other people with respect." (Delia, age 9)

"Knowing that children are more important than gold or silver or one hundred dollar bills." (Kiersten, age 11)

"A community full of people that love you." (Peter, age 10)

WHAT STEPS DO YOU PERSONALLY
TAKE TO MAKE CERTAIN THAT
YOU REMAIN YOUNG-AT-HEART?

"I wrestle with my dad whenever I'm not too busy." (Thomas, age 7)

"I read books with meaning in them like Baseball Hall-of-Famers." (George, age 8)

"Playing with the right dolls..... The kind that, when you pull their string, they tell you you are beautiful and don't work too hard." (Lauren, age 7)

"I read Superman comic books." (Peter, age 10)

"I watch horror movies and they're so ridiculous they make me laugh like a kid again." (Sean, age 10)

"I play 'Pretty Pretty Princess' every chance I get." (Aliya, age 4)

"Festivals and carnivals and Flintstone Vitamins.......
Those are the best things you can do for yourself
if you want to stay young." (Mark, age 8)

"Roller skating takes my mind off school or anything
else I don't like too much." (Hayden, age 9)

"I recommend picnics by a pond to anyone that has
a picnic basket...... But don't forget the napkins or
you'll get jelly on your face." (Ally, age 7)

"We plant trees so the world looks prettier in my neighborhood --
and then you feel good inside too." (Jenny, age 8)

"It's getter harder every year to be young-at-heart...... I
turn the big one-one next year." (Bruce, age 10)

"I don't have to do anything special to be young-at-heart.......
I'm a kid. It comes naturally to me." (Bogdan, age 10)

WHAT LIFE LESSONS HAVE YOU
ACQUIRED IN YOUR CHILDHOOD THAT
YOU THINK WILL BE VALUABLE
FOR REMAINING YOUNG-AT-HEART
LATER ON?

"How to make friends and keep them." (Sam, age 8)

"How to tell the difference between somebody who is a true friend and somebody who just says they are." (Samantha, age 10)

"How it's not always a good idea to wear a watch and be thinking of the time." (Jeffrey, age 11)

"To not be selfish and share my toys...... It's a big part of my success." (John, age 8)

"How to put my clothes on by myself...... If somebody else had to do it later on, it could cause a whole bunch of trouble." (Gary, age 5)

"How to talk and read and read a map and do the things you have to do to get to Disneyworld." (Mark, age 8)

"How to stand on my hands and walk on my own two feet." (Tom, age 11)

"How to spell tough words like 'reconciliation'
and 'gratitude'....." (Ian, age 12)

"I learned how to make a happy family........ That
should be important later on." (Clay, age 8)

"I learned my ABC's and that will keep me young because
that's how I can read picture books." (Ray, age 6)

"Childhood has taught me to sing this song: 'I'll be there
for you...... Yes, I will.....'" (Mary Leigh, age 11)

"All these years have taught me to love pretty much everybody......
Love keeps your heart as young as a kid in preschool!" (Jenny, age 8)

"I have learned that life is short and that it's
important to value every day." (Jared, age 13)

WHY IS IT THAT, REGRETTABLY, SOME ADULTS
FORGET THE LESSONS OF CHILDHOOD
ONCE THEY GROW UP?

"Their minds turn to silly putty after thirty." (Davis, age 9)

"Their memories are bad from workin' too hard." (Donny, age 8)

"They don't go back and remember what it's like
to go in the air on a swing." (Enzo, age 7)

"Because they have dollar signs buzzing around in
their busy heads too much of the day...... The dollar
signs get in the way of life." (Brenda, age 10)

"Sometimes they are too worried about their weight
to be happy and young." (James, age 9)

"Sometimes they're too busy taking care of their kids to take care of themselves..... But you gotta do both to be young-at-heart." (Kelly, age 8)

"Maybe an adult just has too many wives and girlfriends to think about." (Tom, age 11)

"The adults get all closed up and squished like they been in a dryer too long..... It isn't easy for adults to stretch themselves out and relax when they get home." (Bruce, age 10)

"Maybe they just forget because it was a long time ago, and they need a kid to act like a doctor and cure them of being too stuffy." (Alana, age 8)

WHAT IS THE ONE MISTAKE THAT MANY ADULTS MAKE THAT KEEPS THEM FROM BEING YOUNG-AT-HEART MORE OF THE TIME?

"They stop looking for new people to play with." (Aliya, age 4)

"They eat on the run rather than sitting down
and enjoying their meals." (Mira, age 7)

"Divorce is the biggest mistake...... But maybe the
second biggest mistake is marriage!" (Ron, age 10)

"Not living anywhere near an ice-skating rink." (Deidre, age 9)

"Not playing kickball." (Barnes, age 8)

"Not getting enough sleep." (Charlie, age 10)

"Not having enough freedom to live and breathe..... They're always going back n' forth to work." (Tom, age 11)

"They forget to take time out to play checkers." (Carey, age 8)

"They spend too much time raising their voices at their kids when they are just frustrated by life..... They should be more chilled out like us kids." (Richard, age 10)

"Not saying what you really mean to people...... That's a waste of time and causes ulcers." (Harold, age 12)

"Taking your kids to the amusement park but having the wrong attitude..... Like when the dad ends up saying: 'You kids had too much chocolate and now you're wild. This was a big mistake. One of the biggest I have ever made!'" (Carey, age 8)

BUT HAVE NO FEAR, WAYWARD ADULTS,
YOU TOO CAN BE YOUNG-AT-HEART IF YOU MERELY
TAKE THESE REMEDIAL STEPS:

STEP ONE - "Learn how to make car sounds out of the side of your mouth!" (Robbie, age 9)

STEP TWO - "Practice skateboarding twice a week." (Antonio, age 10)

STEP THREE - "Spend a week in kindergarden.... If you can't get into one, try first grade." (Bonnie, age 8)

STEP FOUR - "Wear a Hawaiian shirt to work instead of a business suit." (Doreen, age 9)

STEP FIVE - "The secret is to eat popcorn every night." (Bonnie, age 8)

STEP SIX - "Act like you hate veggies even if
you really don't hate them." (Gil, age 11)

STEP SEVEN - "Move your entire family next to a miniature
golf course..... The ones with the mean giant pirates are
the best. I recommend them." (Dexter, age 10)

STEP EIGHT - "Go to Chuckie Cheese every weekend. But
don't bring your little sister even if she's fifty." (Carey, age 8)

STEP NINE - "Look up in the sky really far away
and see if you can see Plato." (George, age 8)

STEP TEN - "Treat yourself to a purple frisbee
that glows in the dark." (Erica, age 10)

STEP ELEVEN - "Sometime when you are walking down the street, imagine you are the pilot of an airplane and use your arms to show the wings.... All the other people on the street will admire you and want to do it too." (C. Allan, age 8)

STEP TWELVE - "Buy a board game for bored people. Don't buy a cheap one, buy a good one...... Sometimes you have to spend money so you can make big changes." (Dominique. age 11)

STEP THIRTEEN - "Play with seven year-olds every chance you get. Pay them to play with you if you have to." (Harry, age 7)

MORE ADVANCED STEPS FOR
GROWNUPS WHO ARE
VERY COMMITTED TO
BEING YOUNG-AT-HEART

ADVANCED STEP ONE - "Never fight or argue with other people if you can help it." (Evan, age 9)

ADVANCED STEP TWO - "Talk to animals and ask them about their feelings." (Melinda, age 6)

ADVANCED STEP THREE - "When you fall down, get yourself up..... And remember that a few scratches aren't going to keep you from doing something fun." (Danny, age 9)

ADVANCED STEP FOUR - "Be friendly to the people you meet and you'll feel younger in your heart." (Barbara, age 10)

ADVANCED STEP FIVE - "Make sure you have a happy childhood to begin with. But even if you didn't, let other people teach you how to be happy like a kid! (Rob, age 11)

WHAT ADULT MEMBER OF YOUR OWN FAMILY ACTS THE MOST YOUTHFUL?

"My father...... My mother says he acts like a baby." (Mark, age 8)

"My Uncle Jim....... He still collects baseball cards and tries to cheat me in the trades." (Trevor, age 10)

"My ninety year-old grandpa. He walks a lot and plays Lucky-Sevens with dice." (Gil, age 11)

"My mother. She sings all the time. Like yesterday, she was singing "On Top of Old Smokey Where Nobody Goes!" (Rose, age 9)

"It's a tie between all the relatives who still ride bicycles." (Mary Leigh, age 10)

"Mom....... She takes her shoes off no matter where we are...... Even in a museum!" (Alana, age 8)

"My Aunt Penny........ She reminds me of a kid because she has freckles and looks funny." (Emma, age 8, names changed to protect the poor aunt)

"My cousin Kenny. He's almost nineteen and he tells me ghost stories so I can't sleep. He's cool." (Damon, age 10

"My brother. He evens talks to his computer and calls it 'Mike'." (Stephanie, age 9)

"My aunt Wendy takes us waddling in the creek because she remembers that kids don't always get all the creek time they need." (Amy, age 10)

"Mom..... She's adventurous and likes to do things like zip-lining." (Jared, age 13)

"My dog Zeke..... He doesn't let a lot of dog years keep him from acting like a kid-at- heart!" (Sebastian, age 11)

**DO YOU THINK MEN OR WOMEN ARE MORE
INCLINED TO BE YOUNG-AT-HEART?**

"It must be ladies because they wear their hearts
right on their dresses." (Justin, age 6)

"Men are rugged in the way they look, and some of them are
slobs, but most of them are soft underneath." (Kali, age 11)

"The dads are more young-at-heart because they
give better piggyback rides!" (Larry, age 7)

"Ladies act younger because they start having fun tea
parties with their dolls and then they keep on doing
it until they're a hundred!" (Robyn, age 7)

"The men I know don't like to order pizza with stuff on it....
They're afraid, just like real little kids." (Ellen, age 9)

"Women are more young-at-heart at jewelry stores; men
are more old and cranky there!" (Emma, age 9)

"Most of the men act younger watching sports...... You would never guess that some of them hold down responsible jobs." (Sarah, age 12)

"I think it's even..... The women shrivel up sooner but the men get larger stomachs faster." (Arnold, age 7)

"It's hard to say which is more young-at-heart, it kind of depends on the personality.... But trust me, I can tell you from lots of experience that girls are determined to look young at all costs, and they would make a pact with the Devil to do it!" (Gil, age 11)

"Men act younger...... The women get old watching too many shows like Dr. Phil." (Bruce, age 10)

"They both might try to get plastic surgery but they don't realize that it makes them look like plastic people." (Jeri Ann, age 11)

"It doesn't matter whether you are a man or a woman. As long as you have construction paper and lots of good markers, especially different shades of blue and red, you can be young-at-heart." (Marianne, age 7)

**IF YOU ARE A YOUNG-AT-HEART PERSON
MOST OF THE TIME, WHAT WILL
THAT TEACH YOU?**

"That it feels good to be in nature and it feels good to walk in the grass with your bare feet." (Emma, age 9)

"That's simple. It teaches you to whistle while you work." (John, age 8)

"It teaches you to play games and not care so much who wins or who loses." (Maureen, age 9)

"It teaches you to wear pink shoes every now and then." (Samantha, age 10)

"It teaches you how much fun it is to go fishing with your own son or daughter; and it teaches you to put the fish back so they can go back to school." (Glenn, age 7)

"It teaches you to say 'Gesundheit' even when a dog sneezes!" (Wayne, age 9)

"It shows you that old-at-heart is something to watch out for...... Don't fall into that old trap." (Barbara, age 10)

"It teaches you about nature and how you should learn nature's rules, and not act like a sloppy spoiled brat when you have a picnic near the water." (Beth, age 11)

"It reminds you not to waste any days in your life because every day is a chance to have fun and enjoy your life." (Naomi, age 11)

"Having a young-at-heart attitude just teaches you to be the kid in you." (Tyler, age 12)

"It teaches you that you can take control over your own life and it doesn't have to be dictated by what other people say." (Jared, age 13)

**WHAT EXACTLY DOES THE WORLD
LOOK LIKE WHEN YOU ARE
YOUNG-AT-HEART?**

"Like you are on the inside of a snowglobe
having a good ol' time!" (Greg, age 12)

"Something like a big theme park where the rides all
have something to do with love." (Damon, age 10)

"It looks like a world where an eleven year-old is the
best candidate to be President." (Tom, age 11)

"The world would be like a big stage where you can show
off how good you are at juggling." (Ron, age 10)

"It looks like a fun place to be a human being because we get to eat
all kinds of things -- not just coconuts and bananas!" (Lara, age 10)

"The fuddy-duddy part of the world that acts old looks silly to you...... Kind of like robots that are all wound up and just listen to dumb commands like 'do more work!'" (Eleanor, age 9)

"When you are young-at-heart, the world looks exciting and amazing, and you are an explorer like the guys who travelled to the moon or like Columbus...... But you should treat natives better." (Carl, age 9)

"The world would look like a nice piece of cheese..... the kind you love to munch on, not the swiss kind with holes in it. If you are truly young-at-heart, your life won't have many holes in it." (Deandre, age 9)

"The world might even seem more exciting to you than a snow day off from school does..... or at least a tie." (Adam, age 7)

"The world looks like a nice and friendly place to live—for you, for me, and for pretty much everybody else I can think of." (Janice, age 10)

WHAT DOES A YOUNG-AT-HEART PERSPECTIVE TEACH YOU ABOUT THE PURPOSE OF LIFE?

"The purpose is simple. Share and care. That's it." (Michelle, age 8)

"We should be young-at-heart because that's
the way God is." (Carey, age 8)

"Our purpose is to help people who are not young-
at-heart be in less pain." (Jenny, age 8)

"You should never grow up, if you can help it." (Mark, age 8)

"The purpose is to have lots of children...... Those houses are
the happiest. They are young-at-heart homes." (Carol, age 9)

"It teaches you to get training in life...... Like if you learn about
riding a bicycle, that teaches you about balance." (C. Allan, age 8)

"Don't take things too seriously. Most problems will give you indigestion, and having indigestion isn't your purpose in life. It's probably something else, but you won't be able to find it if you have indigestion." (Peter, age 10)

"Life is about having a popsicle on a sunny day...... That can teach you a lot about the simple things." (Jeanne, age 9)

"The purpose of life is forgetting about whether you are young or old. It's about being the absolute best kid or grownup you can be." (Nathaniel, age 13)

"Our purpose is to be young-at-heart at least two big times -- at the beginning of life and at the end...... The rest of the time just do the best you can." (Ginny, age 12)

"We were just put here because God loves us like children. But while we are visiting here, we should have hearts like children do—caring so much about the world and about making the world a happy place." (Lily, age 11)

"The purpose is different for everyone........ But maybe being
young-at-heart helps you see God better -- like you just put on
a brand new pair of looking glasses." (Fernando, age 12)

FAMILIAR THOUGHTS TO ALL THOSE
WHO COUNT THEMSELVES AMONG THE VERY
YOUNG-AT-HEART:
"FAIRY TALES CAN TRUE,............"

"They are coming to a three-story house near you." (Gil, age 11)

"Fairy tales can come true, especially if you live in the
land of the red, white and blue." (Stephen, age 13)

"They can even happen to a grownup like you!" (Evan, age 9)

"But you will probably have to work real hard to
make it happen for you." (Joanna, age 10)

"They only come true if you give the fairy godmother
a present on her birthday." (Samantha, age 10)

"You got a better chance of them coming true if you
never stop acting like a child." (Jocelyn, age 11)

"But before they can come true you have to wish for them like anything -- and it doesn't hurt to have powerful connections in powerful places either." (Tom, age 11)

"I think they can come true, but I am only six, so I just get them read to me mostly." (Stan, age 6)

"Before they can come true, you have to pass the young-at-heart test, and do something like kiss people for no special reason." (Eleanor, age 9)

"Fairy tales can come true for sure if you think like a kid, and you act like one too!" (Maureen, age 8)

"Fairy tales aren't just for kids. They can come true but you gotta believe that people can fly and other stuff like that, and a lot of adults aren't too into that." (Jan, age 8)

"They can come true if you are young-at-heart -- especially because then every day will bring you some interesting and new." (Lynn, age 12)

"Fairy tales can come true if you dedicate yourself
to it and set your mind to it." (Jared, age 13)

"ALL THAT YOU NEED TO BE YOUNG-AT-HEART IS ...."

"An imagination and an ability to dream." (Kera, age 13)

"A sandbox filled with friends." (Holly, age 6)

"A smile on your face and a friendly attitude
toward the world." (Ethan, age 12)

"Being really comfortable with playing with kids." (Benny, age 6)

"All you need to be young-at-heart is a lemonade stand and
another kid to fill in for you if you get tired." (Cole, age 8)

"Just avoid dog mess..... That will put you in a better mood and keep
you young-at-heart and keep your shoes clean too." (Kelly, age 8)

"A jump rope....... and maybe a lot of jumping
ability in your legs." (Claire, age 9)

"To play on a soccer team and be a part of something
that's bigger than you alone." (Carey, age 8)

"Swim in a lake in the winter..... That will get your
heart feeling really young again." (Gil, age 11)

"You want to be young-at-heart? Then just try to remember
when you were in your playpen and your mother thought
you were God's gift to the planet!" (Lisa, age 11)

"The biggest thing is hanging around kids....... All you really need
is a kid to remind you how to be young-at-heart." (Tom, age 11)

"All you need to be young-at-heart is winning two million dollars
in the lottery and giving half of it to charity." (Deborah, age 13)

"A good book and a good hammock." (Charlie, age 13)

'All you need to be young-at-heart is the belief
that you can be." (Jared, age 13)

"A peaceful heart." (Jennifer, age 12)

ON THE NATURE OF A YOUTHFUL HEART

"You don't take the moonlight and stars for granted." (Kelly, age 11)

"You just care about happiness, and you don't care so much if someone combed their hair the neatest." (Carl, age 9)

"Young hearts get hurt easy but they bounce back quick like kids do." (Patricia, age 9)

"Those young hearts like to ride on swan boats..... and the swans must be young-at-heart too because they get all excited when the people on the boats take their picture." (Lorie, age 7)

"Young hearts do not have any big hangups..... They just breathe in life." (Elizabeth, age 11)

"No matter how important or how old you are, what is really important about being young-at-heart is that no matter what happens, the beat goes on." (Eric, age 13)

"Young hearts always have hope; they figure things can always get better." (Rosemary, age 8)

"If you are a young-at-heart-heart kind of person, you are always the first one to see a rainbow." (Carly, age 11)

"If a person is young-at-heart I think they might feel closer to God." (Bethany, age 10)

"There is no heart more wonderful than a young heart." (Kimberly, age 13)

"The more I think about it, the youngest people and the oldest people like my grandma are the most young-at-heart........ The people in-between need to listen and learn from the children and the grandmas." (George, age 12)

"The more joy you have in your heart, the younger it will feel." (Tom, age 10)

"Everyone makes a decision if you want to be playful or just stuck in the mud...... So it is up to you if you want to truly be young-at-heart." (Gina, age 12)

"The key is not letting other people tell you what you can and can't do. Being young-at-heart helps you to realize that you can make your own life be the way you want it to be." (Jared, age 13)